STEAMPUNK

DESIGNS

Marty Noble

Dover Publications, Inc.
Mineola, New York

Note

The detailed plates in this unique coloring collection will transport you to an era of clockwork gadgetry, gizmos, and stream-powered machines. Use your imagination as you color images of society men and women elegantly adorned with mechanical accessories, mad scientists showing off their steam-powered blasters, inventors alongside their flight-machines and other transport devices, plus many more.

Copyright

Copyright © 2013 by Dover Publications, Inc.
All rights reserved.

Bibliographical Note

Steampunk Designs is a new work, first published by
Dover Publications, Inc., in 2013.

International Standard Book Number

ISBN-13: 978-0-486-49919-2
ISBN-10: 0-486-49919-7

Manufactured in the United States by Courier Corporation
49919702   2013
www.doverpublications.com

STEAMPUNK